STINKY PUPPY
ADVENTURES

Stinky Puppy Adventures: Where's The Roast Beef?

ISBN 978-1-0689843-1-0

Published by Nestled in the Woods Publishing Inc.
www.nestledinthewoodspublishinginc.ca

Second Edition: September 2024

STINKY PUPPY ADVENTURES

WHERE'S THE ROAST BEEF?

2nd Edition

MELANIE HORNIK

Grandpapa cooked a yummy roast beef. Stinky Puppy was so excited.

"Now, you'll have to wait until it cools," Grandpapa gently explained.

"Well . . . ," thought Stinky Puppy, "if I can't have roast beef, then I might as well go outside and have some fun."

Stinky Puppy loved to play ball, but Mr. Longbottom, the neighbour next door wouldn't share.

"Hey! I'll take that." Stinky Puppy yelped.

Wanting to be helpful, he tried to collect the mail, but the mailman ran away.

"Maybe there's treasure to be found?" wondered Stinky Puppy. He decided he'd have to dig to find out. What fun!

WOOF!

He even tried to convince a squirrel to come down from the tree to play with him. Who doesn't love a good game of chase?" Stinky Puppy wondered.

Stinky Puppy's tummy began to rumble with hunger. It was then that he remembered . . . .

THE ROAST
BEEF!

"I've got to get home!" Stinky Puppy roared. He ran as fast as his little legs could carry him.

Stinky Puppy burst into the kitchen only to find that the roast beef was gone!

He searched in the pantry, but the roast beef couldn't be found.

Stinky Puppy hoped it was under his bed, but it wasn't.

"I'll check the garage!" he said. Stinky Puppy searched every nook and cranny, but he couldn't find it.

He searched high...

and he searched low.

"I can't find that warm, juicy, delicious roast beef anywhere!" Stinky Puppy yelped. It was time to ask Grandpapa for help.

Stinky Puppy ran in search of the loving old man in hopes that he would know what to do.

He raced through the house looking for Grandpapa

Stinky Puppy found him sitting in the dining room with the roast beef.

Stinky Puppy was relieved! The roast beef wasn't missing after all. Grandpapa even had a plate ready for him to eat too.

Let Nestled in the Woods Publishing Inc. be your trusted publisher of children's books and educational resources.
www.nestledinthewoodspublishinginc.ca
Adventure Awaits in the Woods
Nestled in the Woods
Publishing Inc.

Printed in Great Britain
by Amazon

53706802R00021